Open Hearts
An Adoption Story

Written by: DeAnna Gallardo

Illustrated by: Audrey Sherlock

WestBow Press books may be ordered through booksellers or by contacting:

WestBow Press
A Division of Thomas Nelson & Zondervan
1663 Liberty Drive
Bloomington, IN 47403
www.westbowpress.com
1 (866) 928-1240

Illustrations by Audrey Sherlock.

ISBN: 978-1-9736-7448-1 (sc)
ISBN: 978-1-9736-7449-8 (e)

Library of Congress Control Number: 2019913672

Print information available on the last page.

WestBow Press rev. date: 10/10/2019

WESTBOW
PRESS®
A DIVISION OF THOMAS NELSON
& ZONDERVAN

To Wadlay may you always
know how loved you are.
love, Mommy

To my adopted friends.
- Audrey Sherlock

We prayed for you many
days and nights before
we knew your name.
For many days, weeks
and even years we played
the waiting game.

Our hearts were open
and excited to see
our family grow,
but the process to adopt
you was very very slow.

Finally the day came
and we saw your photo
for the first time.
we fell in love instantly
and thanked God for the
blessing of a lifetime.

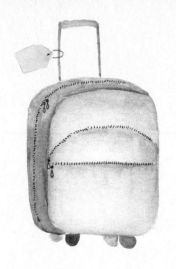

We packed our bags and
began the journey to finally
meet you face to face.
we were so excited it was
all we could do to keep our
hearts at a steady pace.

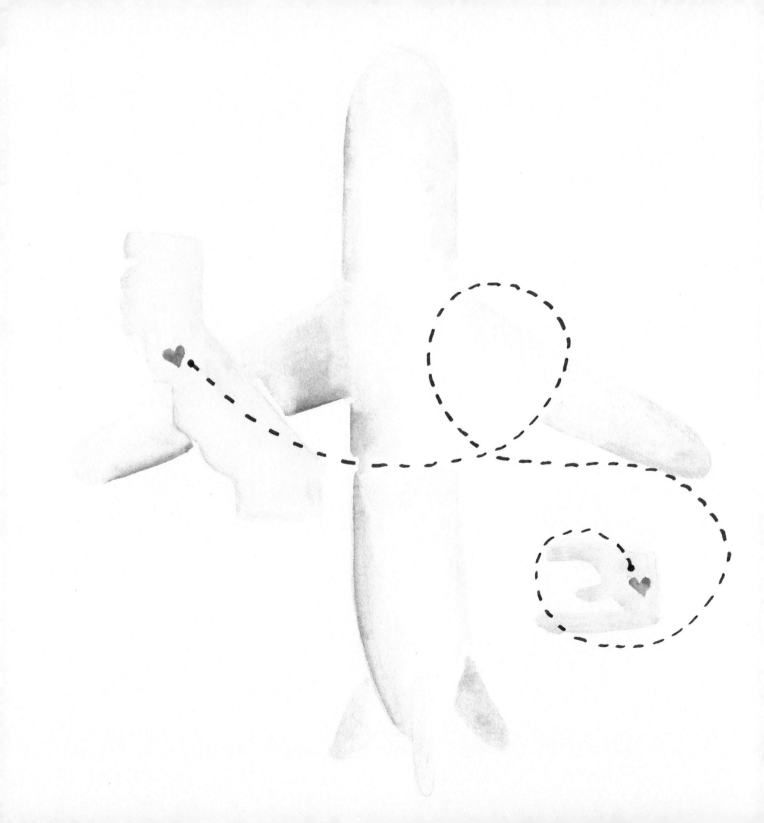

We know you must be scared
and may not understand,
we promise to take care
of you, keep you safe, and
hold your little hand.

HELLO
my name is

When the moment finally
came and we finally held
you in our arms,
we knew our family
was complete with all
your little charms.

We stood in awe of the miracle you are and the very special treasure. the joy in our hearts we felt in that moment. we could never measure.

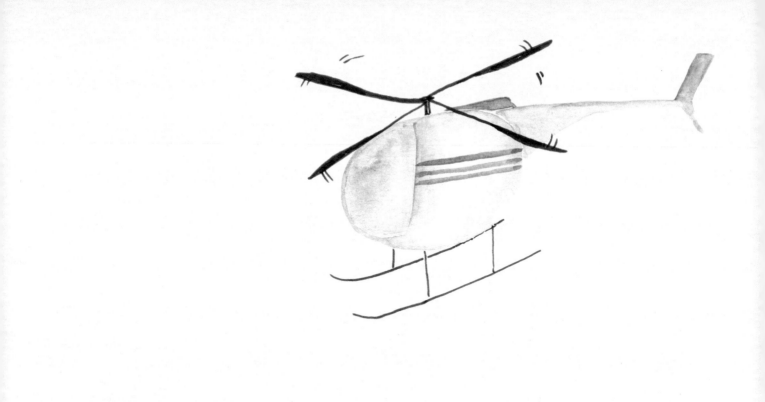

Now it is time to leave
together and start the
long journey home.
We promise to stay with
you and keep you close
so you dont feel alone.

There will be many new exciting things to experience this day, new foods, new smells, new sights to see all along the way.

And when we finally arrive
at home there will be friends
and family to meet.
this moment is sure to
be very very sweet.

The ones you see may have
tears in their eyes,
but dont be afraid their hearts
have just grown in size.

For you are a blessing far greater
than we ever could have imagined.
a blessing through prayers and
love that has finally happened.

The gift you are to all of us
is one only from above,
the gift that you are is
such a great gift of love.

DeAnna Gallardo is a wife, mother of three and lover of all things peanut butter.

Audrey Sherlock is a high schooler, loves art and snacks.